CHRISTIAN
FESTIVALS AND TRADITIONS

by Mari Bolte

PEBBLE
a capstone imprint

Published by Pebble, an imprint of Capstone
1710 Roe Crest Drive, North Mankato, Minnesota 56003
capstonepub.com

Copyright © 2025 by Capstone. All rights reserved. No part of this publication may
be reproduced in whole or in part, or stored in a retrieval system, or transmitted
in any form or by any means, electronic, mechanical, photocopying, recording, or
otherwise, without written permission of the publisher.

Library of Congress Cataloging-in-Publication Data is available
on the Library of Congress website.
ISBN: 9780756594572 (hardcover)
ISBN: 9780756594626 (paperback)
ISBN: 9780756594619 (ebook PDF)

Summary: Readers curious about world religions can explore the meaning
and customs behind major Christian holidays and traditions, including Advent,
Christmas, and Easter.

Editorial Credits
Designer: Dina Her; Media Researcher: Jo Miller; Production Specialist: Tori Abraham

Image Credits
Bridgeman Images: Fred de Noyelle/Godong, 17; Getty Images: FG Trade, 26,
GMVozd, 1, 14, NurPhoto, 12, Philippe Lissac /GODONG, 18, Spencer Platt, 7,
urbazon, 21; Shutterstock: Adam Jan Figel, 8, Atitude, background (throughout),
Dmitriy Feldman svarshik, 23, Natalia Ruedisueli, 19, Pit Stock, cover (top), pon
piriya, 29, Pressmaster, 15, Renata Sedmakova, 5, 11, sweet marshmallow, 25,
Tatjana Baibakova, cover (bottom)

Any additional websites and resources referenced in this book are not maintained,
authorized, or sponsored by Capstone. All product and company names are
trademarks™ or registered® trademarks of their respective holders.

Printed and bound in China. 6098

TABLE OF CONTENTS

Introduction to Christianity.................4

Ash Wednesday and Lent...................6

Holy Week... 10

All Saints' Day.................................... 16

Advent 18

Christmas 20

Life Events... 24

Glossary 30

Read More 31

Internet Sites.................................. 31

Index.. 32

About the Author 32

Words in **bold** are in the glossary.

INTRODUCTION TO CHRISTIANITY

Christianity is the most common religion in the world. Nearly 2.5 billion people share the belief in one God. They read the same Holy Bible. They celebrate shared culture, customs, and holidays.

Christians believe God created the world and everything on it. He sent his son, Jesus Christ, to Earth. Jesus would be the link between Heaven and humanity. He shared the word of God. Acting as a role model, he said people should love and forgive one another.

Jesus experienced suffering and **temptation** alongside people. Even when faced with challenges, Jesus did not give up. His death and **resurrection** showed that true believers could live forever.

There are multiple branches of Christianity. The largest are Roman Catholic and Protestant.

Ash Wednesday and Lent

Most Christian holidays fall on the same day every year. They use the 12-month Gregorian calendar. However, Easter and the holy days leading up to it use the lunar calendar. That means that the dates move around, depending on the moon's phases.

On Ash Wednesday, Christians receive a blessing. A priest marks a person's forehead with ashes. The ashes symbolize **penance** and prayer. Some Christians eat only one simple meal on Ash Wednesday. **Fasting** is a way to show discipline.

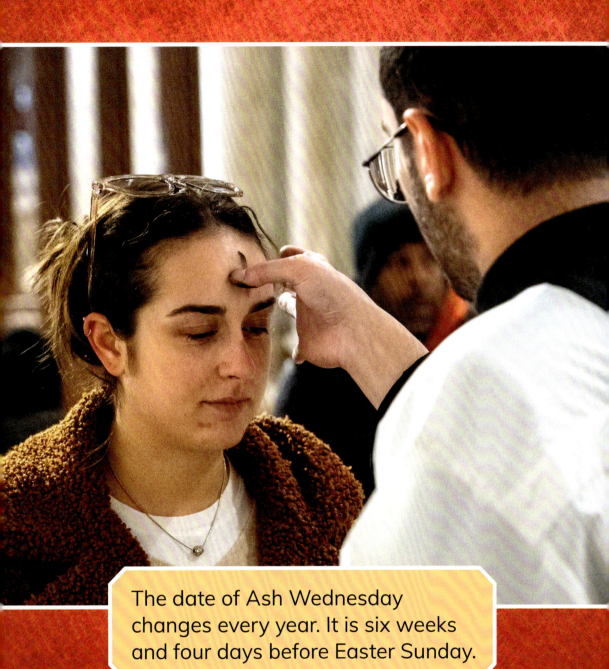

The date of Ash Wednesday changes every year. It is six weeks and four days before Easter Sunday.

Jesus was tempted by the devil.

Ash Wednesday begins the 40 days of Lent. Lent symbolizes the 40 days Jesus spent fasting in the desert and resisting sin, or actions that go against the word of God.

Christians remember Jesus's battle by fasting, praying, and giving money to the poor. Christians fast on Ash Wednesday and Good Friday.

Some Christians give up something they enjoy during Lent. They may give up sugary drinks or candy. On Fridays, they do not eat meat. These sacrifices bring them closer to God.

HOLY WEEK

The Sunday before Easter is Palm Sunday. It marks the day Jesus arrived in Jerusalem. Palm branches are used in churches to symbolize the branches waved by the welcoming crowd.

The Thursday before Easter is called Maundy Thursday. Christians remember Jesus's Last Supper, the final meal he shared with his **disciples**. Some churches have special **Masses** or services. Anyone who has been baptized is given wine and bread, which symbolize the blood and body of Christ.

Jesus washed the feet of his followers as an act of service. Some churches have foot-washing ceremonies to remind people that everyone is equal.

The word *Maundy* comes from the Latin word for "commandment." It symbolizes Jesus's commandment to serve others.

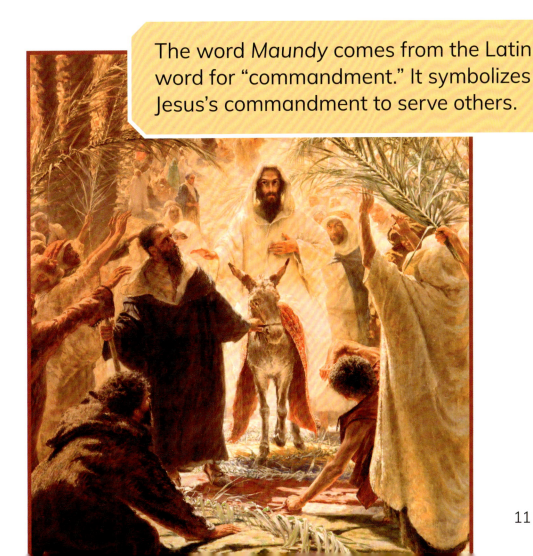

People attend a Good Friday service in Poland.

Good Friday is the next day. It is an observance of Jesus's **crucifixion**. Christians believe that Jesus died to save people from their sins. They spend this day mourning and praying. Churches hold special Good Friday services. There are no decorations at the front of the church.

After services, families spend time together. Some use resurrection eggs to help children understand the Easter story. Eggs symbolize new life and Jesus's resurrection. A dozen plastic eggs hold special objects that symbolize Jesus's journey to the cross.

Christ died on a cross on Good Friday. He was buried for three days. Then Christ was brought back to life on Easter Sunday. Easter is a day of celebration.

Some people make Easter bread. It is a sweet treat with a colorful egg baked into the center.

Decorating eggs dates back as far as the 1200s.

After a special Easter church service that focuses on hope and joy, families get together for a meal. In the United States, parents hide colorful eggs for children to find. In Scandinavia, children go door-to-door asking for eggs and sweets. Ukrainians coat eggs in wax and cover them with detailed designs.

ALL SAINTS' DAY

All Saints' Day is celebrated on November 1. It honors saints who have died. Saints are holy people who have gone to heaven. The Bible says every Christian can be a saint. The Roman Catholic Church recognizes more than 10,000 saints.

In many countries, including the Philippines, Italy, and Haiti, schools and businesses are closed. Families remember their loved ones. They leave flowers or light candles at grave sites.

All Saints' Day is also known as All Hallows' Day.

ADVENT

The word *Advent* means "arrival." Advent begins on the Sunday closest to November 30. It is a period leading up to Christmas Eve. It lasts about four weeks. For most, Advent marks the beginning of the **liturgical** year. It is also called the Christian year.

Advent calendars have a flap for each day that opens to reveal a picture or treat.

In some countries, such as Germany and the United Kingdom, Advent candles are red.

People light candles on the four Sundays during Advent. The candles symbolize hope, peace, joy, and love. Candles are usually violet, but blue, light purple, and pink are also common colors.

CHRISTMAS

Christmas Eve falls on December 24. It is the day before Christmas Day, which celebrates the birth of Jesus. Friends and family give gifts and share food. This symbolizes God's gift, his only Son. The Bible says three wise men visited Jesus later. They brought him gifts too.

Today, many people celebrate Christmas even if they are not Christians. Many schools and businesses close on Christmas Day so people can spend time with their families.

Christmas comes from the words "Christ's Mass."

Christmas is celebrated around the world. Homes and evergreen trees are decorated with lights.

Some traditions are older than the actual holiday. People in Scandinavia lighted trees to brighten their homes during winter **solstice**. Other people in Europe burned a Yule log to mark the year's shortest day.

Over time, these acts became part of Christmas. The lights symbolize Jesus, who is sometimes called the "light of the world." Star-topped Christmas trees represent the star that appeared when Jesus was born.

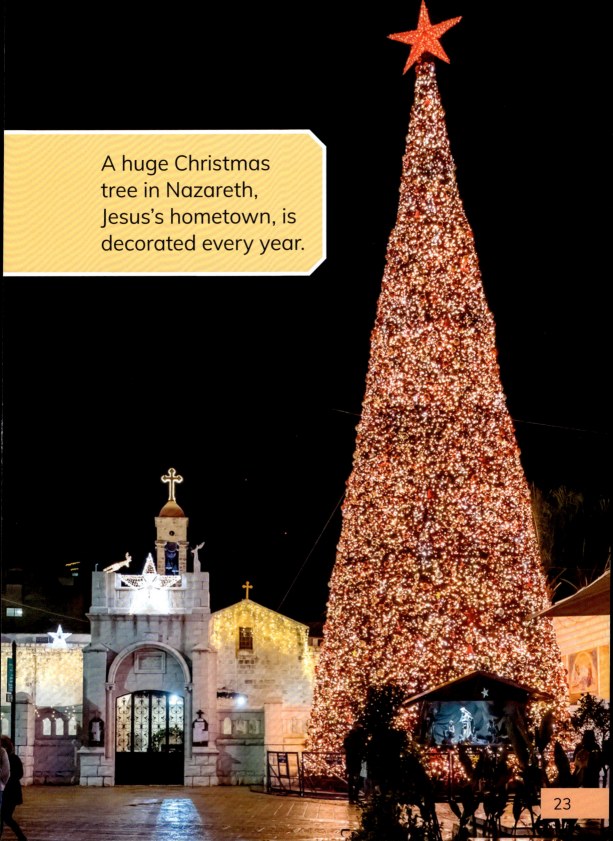

A huge Christmas tree in Nazareth, Jesus's hometown, is decorated every year.

LIFE EVENTS

In some Christian groups, babies are baptized. Friends and family gather at the church. A religious leader, such as a priest, bishop, or **deacon**, sprinkles holy water on the baby. Other groups do not baptize until people are old enough to be full believers.

Funerals usually take place in the church too. Prayers and **sermons** are read. **Hymns** are sung. People take time to remember the person who has died. Then the person is buried in a cemetery.

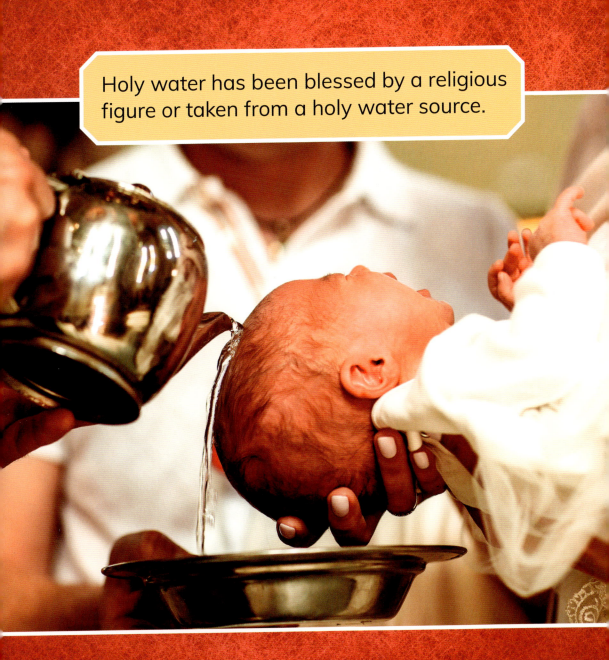

Holy water has been blessed by a religious figure or taken from a holy water source.

Christians believe that marriage was created by God.

Weddings usually take place in a church. A minister or priest reads from the Bible. The couple exchange vows. They promise to love and cherish God and each other. Family and friends witness the marriage.

After the ceremony, guests gather for a meal. Sometimes there is dancing. Gifts help the new couple start a home together.

People who were baptized as babies are usually confirmed when they are young teenagers. They are ready to accept the promises their godparents made during baptism. Adults can be baptized and confirmed at any age.

A religious leader asks the person if they are ready to accept God. Then the leader places their hands on the person's head. A prayer and a blessing are said. The person is now a full member of the church.

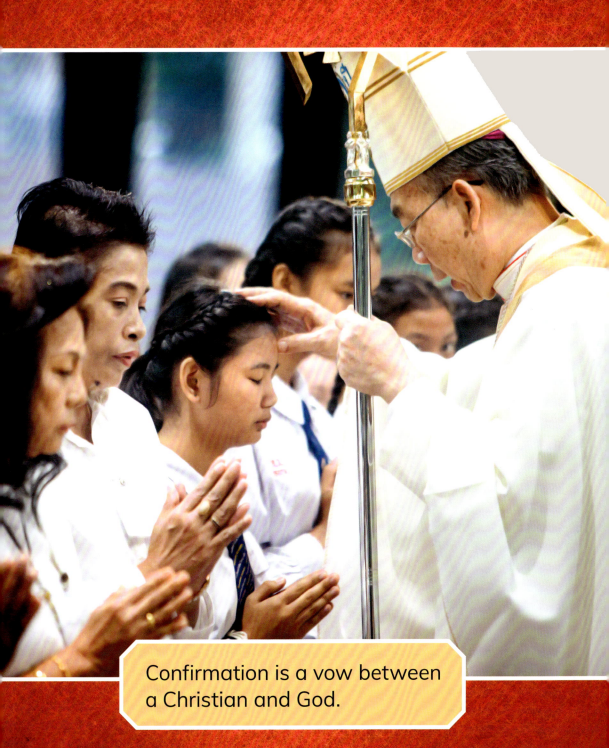

Confirmation is a vow between a Christian and God.

GLOSSARY

crucifixion (kroo-suh-FIK-shuhn)—the execution of a person by nailing or binding them to a cross

deacon (DEE-kuhn)—someone who helps a minister in a Christian church

disciple (duh-SY-puhl)—a devoted follower of a religious or moral teacher

fast (FAST)—to give up eating for a period of time

hymn (HIM)—a religious song or poem

liturgical (lih-TUR-juh-kuhl)—relating to words, music, and actions used in public worship, especially in the Christian religion

Mass (MASS)—a Catholic worship service

penance (PEN-ans)—acts that prove people are sorry for their sins

resurrection (res-uh-REK-shuhn)—the act of coming back to life

sermon (SUR-muhn)—a talk on a religious or moral subject, especially given during a church service

solstice (SOL-stis)—the days with the longest and shortest amounts of daylight

temptation (temp-TAY-shuhn)—the state of being led to do something wrong

READ MORE

Andrews, Elizabeth. *Christianity*. Minneapolis: DiscoverRoo, an imprint of Pop!, 2024.

Kaiser, Emma. *Christmas*. Minneapolis: Abdo Publishing, 2024.

Stewart, Whitney. *What Do You Celebrate?: Holidays and Festivals Around the World*. New York: Union Square Kids, 2023.

INTERNET SITES

BBC Bitesize: What Is Christianity?
bbc.co.uk/bitesize/articles/zvfnkmn

Kiddle: Christianity Facts for Kids
kids.kiddle.co/Christianity

United Religions Initiative: Christianity: Basic Beliefs
uri.org/kids/world-religions/christian-beliefs

INDEX

Advent, 18, 19
All Saints' Day, 16, 17
Ash Wednesday, 6, 7, 9

baptisms, 24, 28
Bible, 4, 16, 20, 27

Christmas, 18, 20, 21, 22, 23
Christmas trees, 22, 23
confirmations, 28, 29

Easter, 6, 7, 10, 13, 14, 15

fasting, 6, 9
foot washing, 11
funerals, 24

Good Friday, 9, 12, 13, 14

Jesus Christ, 4, 5, 8, 9, 10, 11, 13, 20, 22, 23

Lent, 9

marriage, 26, 27
Maundy Thursday, 10

Palm Sunday, 10

temptation, 5

winter solstice, 22

ABOUT THE AUTHOR

Mari Bolte is the author and editor of hundreds of children's books. Every book is her favorite as long as the readers learned something and enjoyed themselves!